For Weston, Theo, and Eli.

If You Find A Forest

Written and Illustrated by Jennifer R. Prost

If you find a forest,

be curious and mindful.

If you find a bird,

listen and observe.

If you find a flower,

breathe in and let go.

If you find a worm,

be gentle and handle with care.

If you find a creek,

identify risk before exploring.

If you find a fawn,

offer space and quietude.

If you find a snail,

rest in the slowness.

If you find a chipmunk,

let wonder guide you.

If you find a nest,

remember how simple and lovely life can be.

Natural Learning Through Nature

Being curious and mindful leads to lifelong learning and awareness of self and surroundings.

Listening and observing leads to strong communication and leadership skills.

Breathing in and letting go leads to mental and physical health and well-being.

Being gentle and handling with care leads to community connection and teamwork.

Identifying risk before exploring leads to informed decision-making and resilience.

Offering space and quietude leads to an appreciation for life and the natural world.

Resting in the slowness leads to stress reduction and emotional regulation practices.

Letting wonder guide you leads to creativity and innovation.

Remembering how simple and lovely life can be leads to reflection and self-reliance.

Jennifer's paintings in this book each represent a special memory from time spent outside with her three young children. It was during those days that she began to notice how many of their needs were being met through unstructured outdoor play. Needs such as physical movement, emotional regulation, rest, and socialization were met while skills associated with academic connections and curiosities were developed through sensory experiences and conversations had within the natural world. It's her hope that families can use this book as encouragement to spend more time together outside.